Content

Who
Lives in a Pond?

Written by Amy Algie   Illustrated by Leonardo Meschini

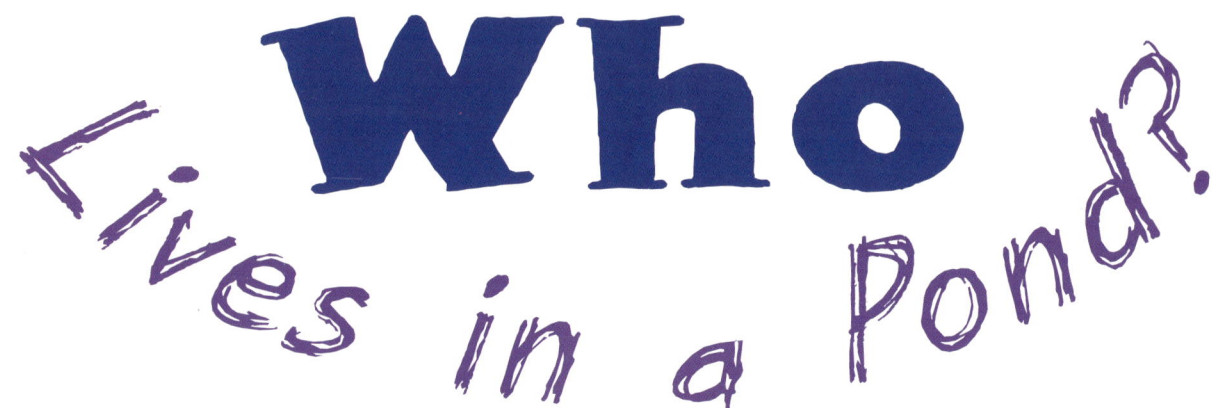

Some birds dive for their dinner.

Ducks and other birds
live in and around ponds.
Some birds eat
plants or insects.
Some birds eat small fish.
They eat tadpoles
and frogs, too.

Can you find me?

3

Frogs and toads
live in and around ponds.
Frogs and toads start
their lives as eggs
in a pond.
Frogs and toads
eat insects.

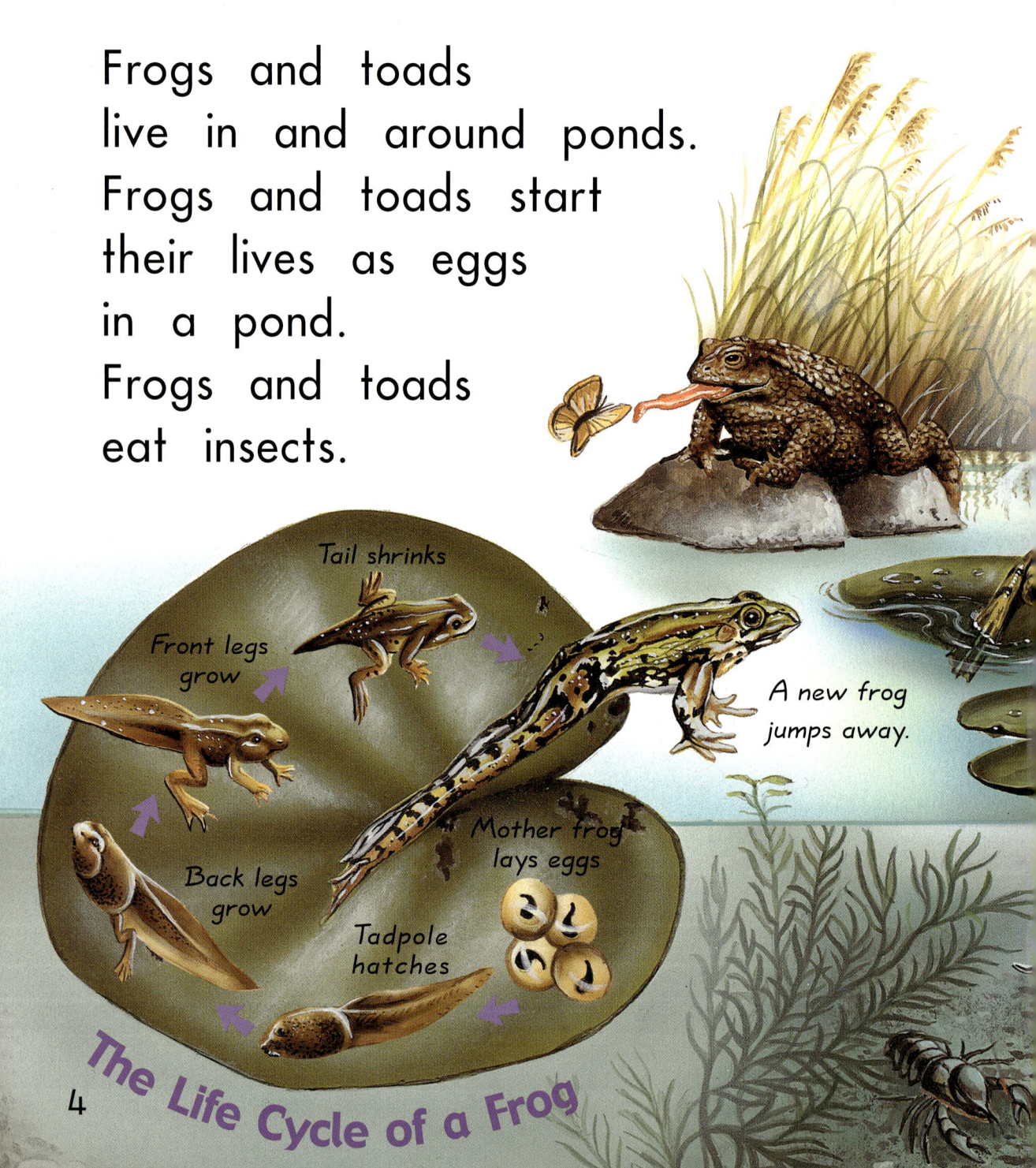

Tail shrinks

Front legs
grow

A new frog
jumps away.

Back legs
grow

Mother frog
lays eggs

Tadpole
hatches

The Life Cycle of a Frog

4

Who is
my mother?

5

Insects live in and around ponds. Mosquitoes and dragonflies start their lives as eggs in a pond.

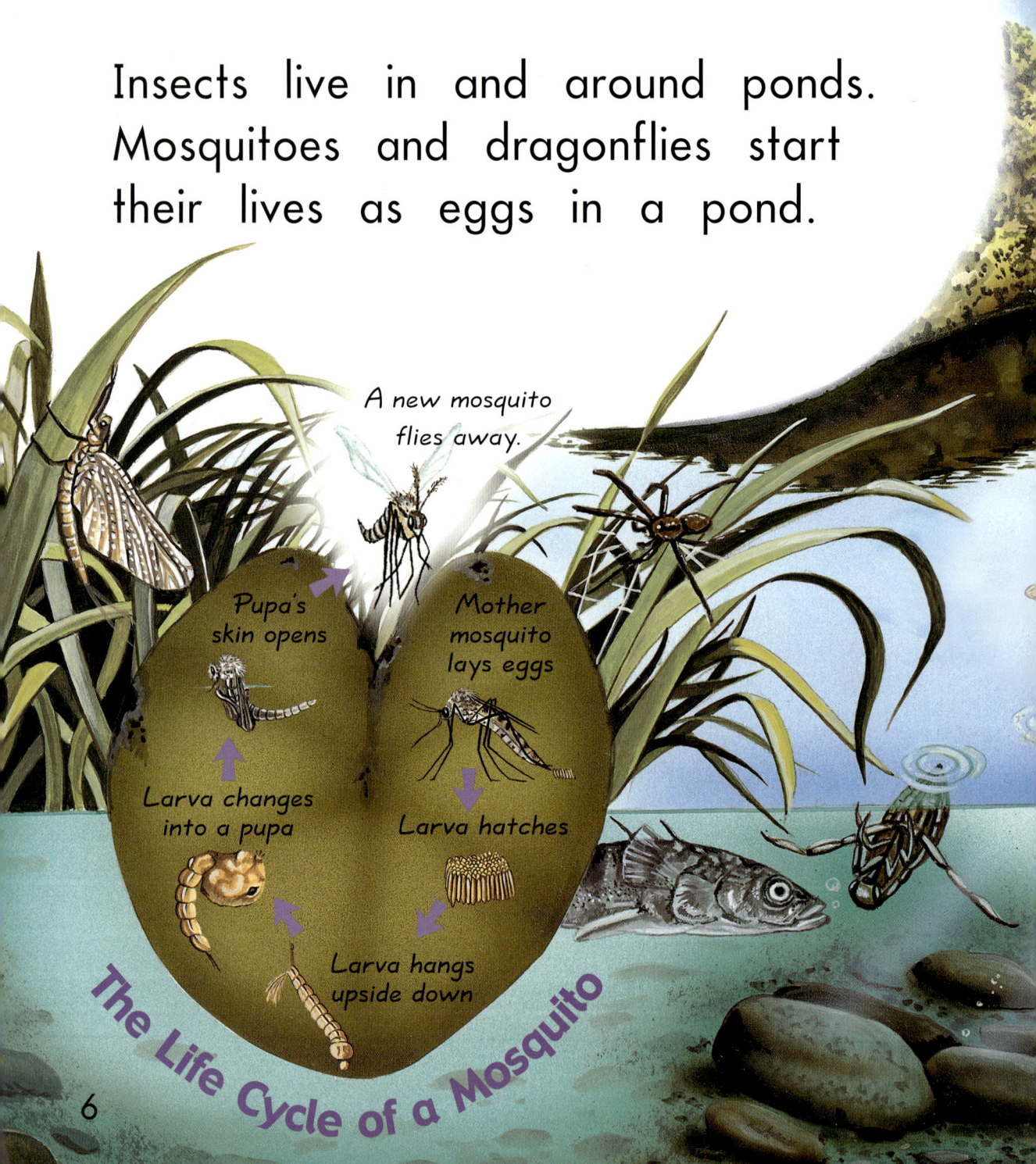

A new mosquito flies away.

Pupa's skin opens

Mother mosquito lays eggs

Larva changes into a pupa

Larva hatches

Larva hangs upside down

The Life Cycle of a Mosquito

Can you
find me?

Turtles live in and around ponds.
Turtles eat insects, plants, and fish.

Snakes live in and around ponds.
Some snakes eat turtle eggs.

The turtle's shell keeps it safe from predators.

How many turtles
can you see?

9

Ugly

Some toads can grow very large. Some are as big as a frisbee!

Some frogs and toads sneak up on prey and hide from their predators.

Some frogs and toads have colours that help them

Some frogs and toads have bright colours that scare away predators.

12

Make a HIP-HOPPER

You will need:

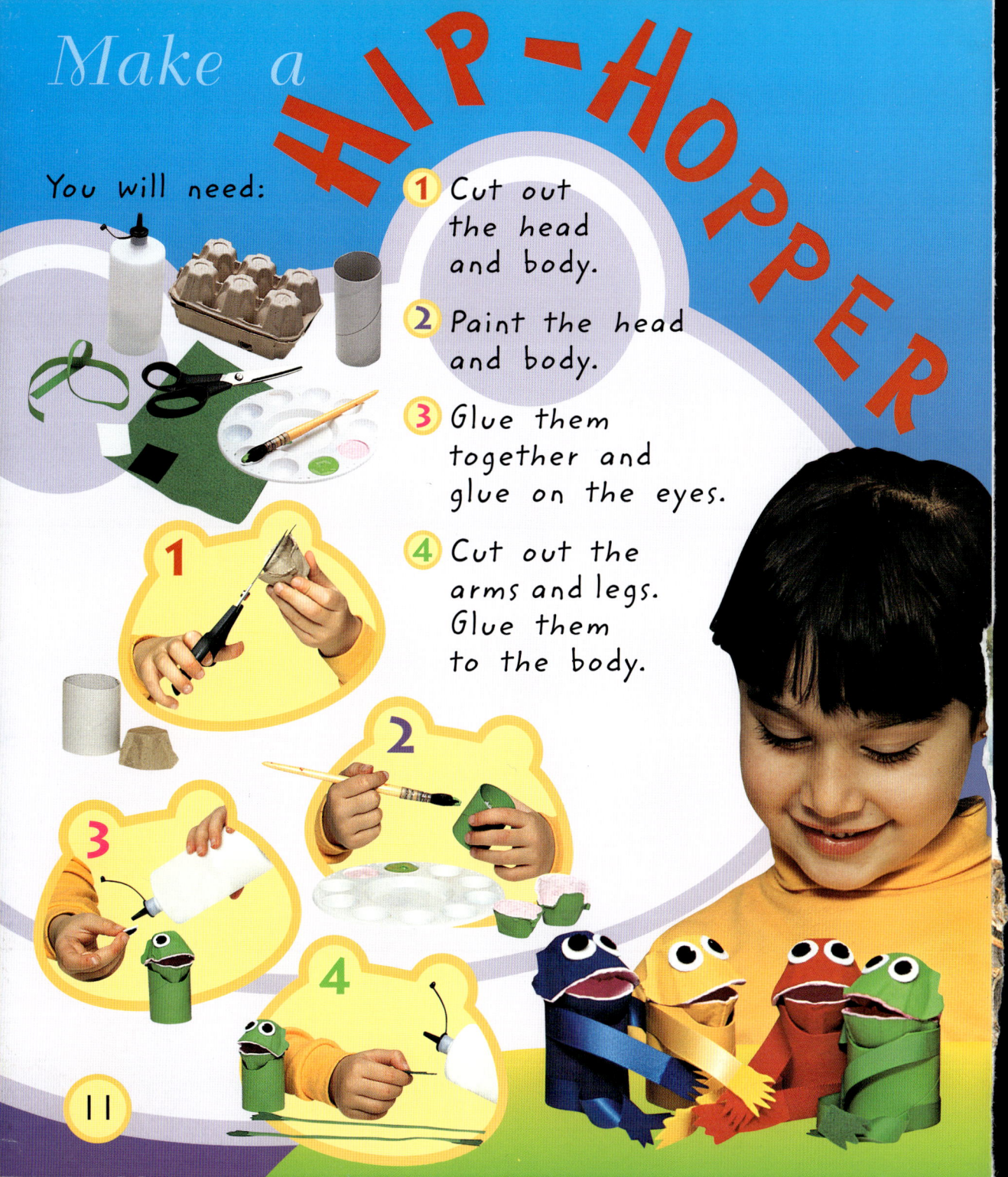

1. Cut out the head and body.

2. Paint the head and body.

3. Glue them together and glue on the eyes.

4. Cut out the arms and legs. Glue them to the body.

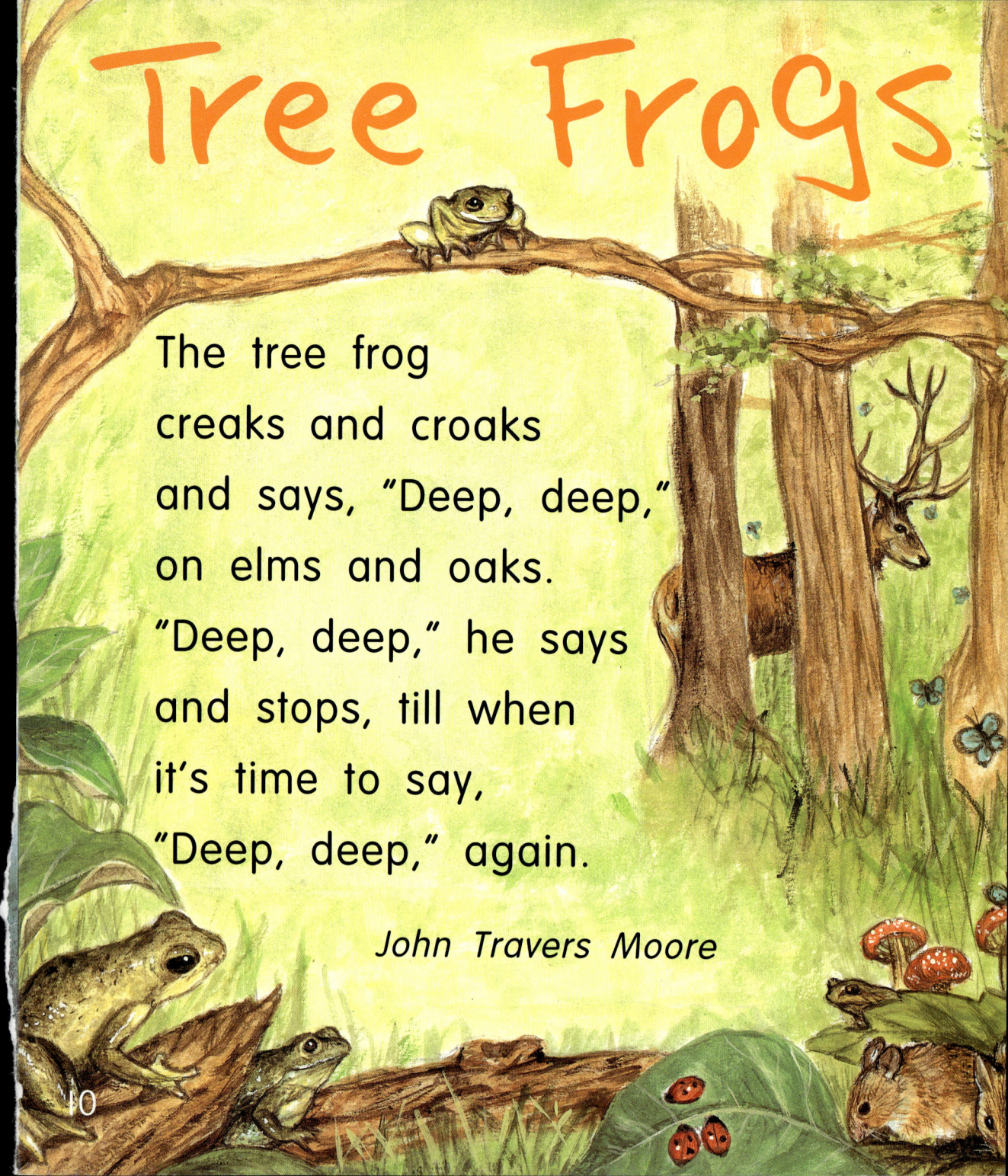

Tree Frogs

The tree frog
creaks and croaks
and says, "Deep, deep,"
on elms and oaks.
"Deep, deep," he says
and stops, till when
it's time to say,
"Deep, deep," again.

John Travers Moore

Froggy Funnies

Q. Why are frogs so happy?

A. They eat whatever bugs them.

Q. What do you get if you cross a frog with a crocodile?

CROAK!

A. A croak-a-dile.

Q. What do frogs eat with hamburgers?

A. French flies.

Q. How does a frog feel with a broken leg?

A. Unhoppy.

Q. What happened to the frog's car when the parking meter expired?

A. It got toad away.

Princes

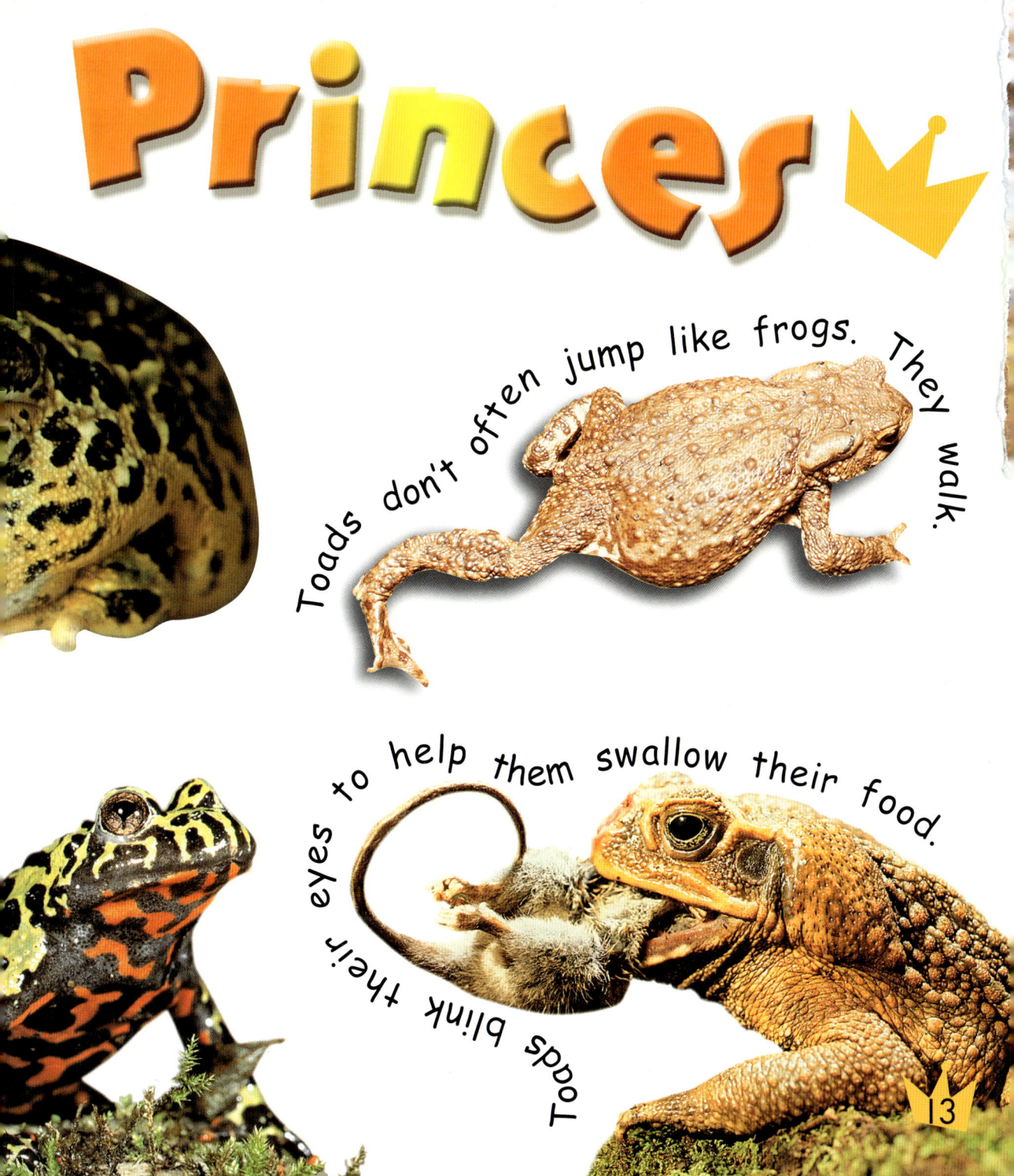

Toads don't often jump like frogs. They walk.

Toads blink their eyes to help them swallow their food.

13

The Frog Prince

A Traditional Story

Illustrated by Lorenzo Van Der Lingen

The Characters

Narrator

Princess

Frog

King

Prince

Narrator: One day,
the king gave the princess
a golden ball.

 **Princess:** Father, I am going to play with my golden ball.

 **King:** Don't go near the well. You may drop your ball into it!

 **Princess:** I will look after it, Father.

 **Narrator:** The princess played with her golden ball.

 **Princess:** Oh no, oh no! My golden ball is in the well.

 **Narrator:** The princess cried and cried.

 **Frog:** Why are you crying, Princess?

 **Princess:** My ball is in the well, and I can't get it. Boo-hoo-hoo!

 **Frog:** I can get it for you. What will you give me in return?

 **Princess:** What do you want?

 **Frog:** I want to be your friend. I want to live with you. If you promise these things, I will get your ball.

 **Princess:** OK, Frog, I promise!

Narrator: *Knock, knock, knock!*

King: Who is at the door?

Princess: Oh no!
It's that ugly frog!

King: What does he want?

Princess: Oh, Father,
my golden ball fell into the well.
The frog got it out for me.
I promised he could be my
friend and live here with us.

King: Then you must keep
your promise.

22

 **Frog:** Pick me up, Princess, and take me to the table.

 **Princess:** Boo-hoo-hoo!

 **Frog:** Give me your plate, Princess, so I can eat.

 **Princess:** Boo-hoo-hoo! Boo-hoo-hoo!

 **Frog:** Now take me to your bedroom, Princess, so I can sleep.

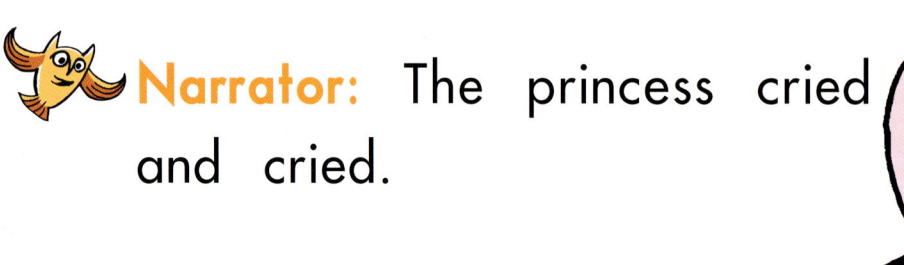 **Narrator:** The princess cried and cried.

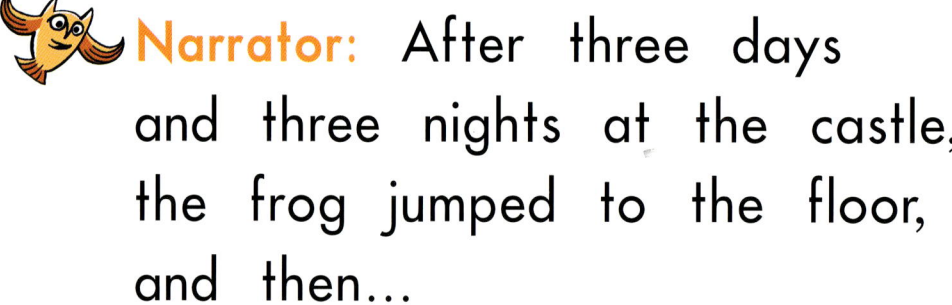 **Narrator:** After three days and three nights at the castle, the frog jumped to the floor, and then…

 **Prince:** Hello, Princess. Surprise!

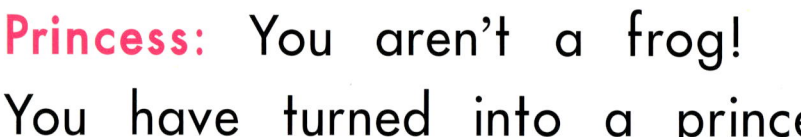 **Princess:** You aren't a frog! You have turned into a prince.

 **Prince:** I was turned into a frog by magic. You helped me. You kept your promise. Thank you, Princess!

 **Princess:** I'm glad I kept my promise. We will be best friends forever!

26

Rainforest

You will need:

15 You stop for a passing sloth. Miss a turn.

14

13

16

17

Start

1

2

3

12 You catch a monkey ride. Leap forward 5 spaces.

11

10 You slip in the mud. Jump back 1 space.

4 You stop for a tarantula. Jump back to start.

9

8

5

6

7 You eat and run. Leap forward 4 spaces.

28

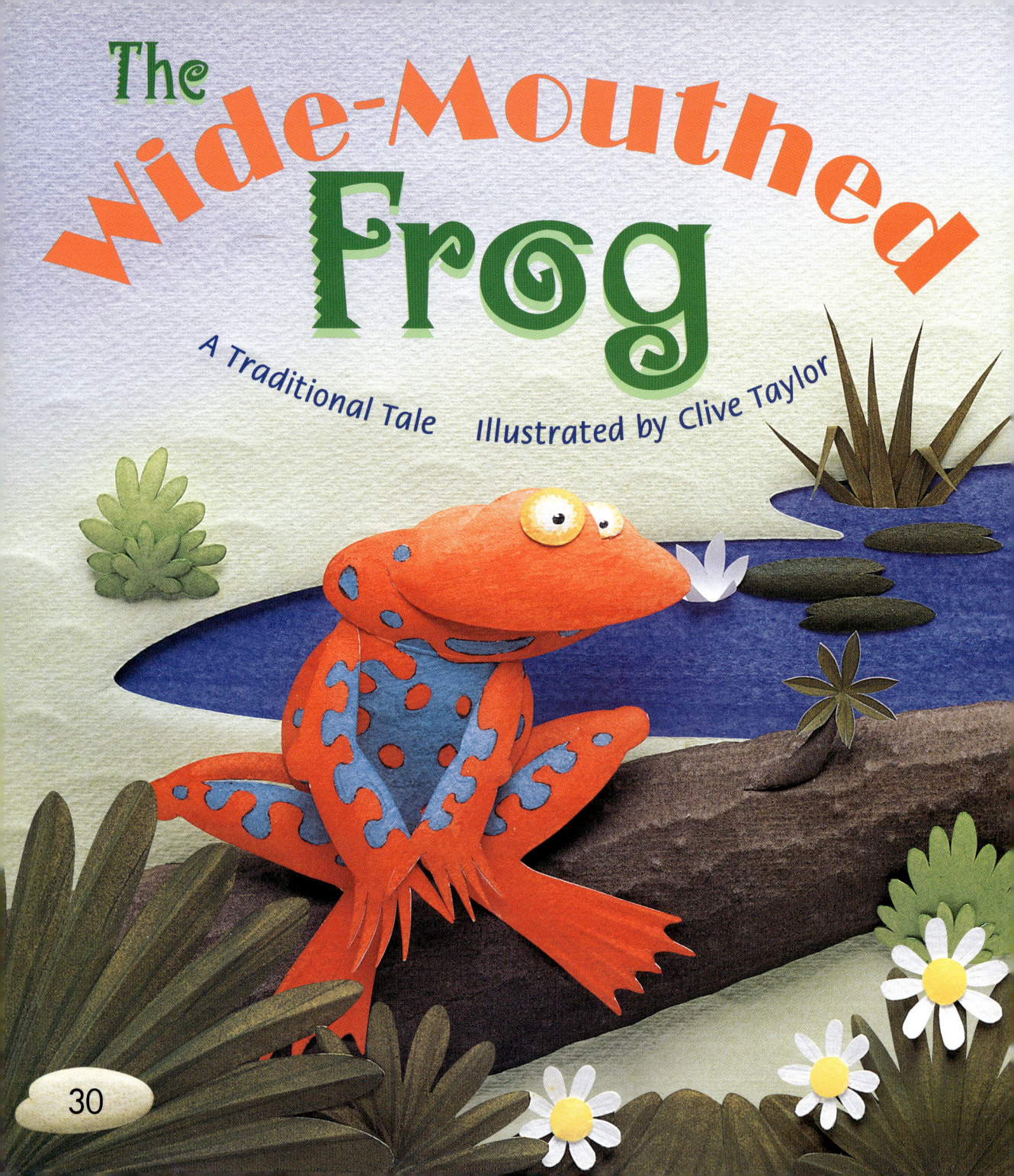

The Wide-Mouthed Frog

A Traditional Tale   Illustrated by Clive Taylor

30

One day,

a wide-mouthed frog

was sitting on a log.

Along came a *butterfly.*

Hello, who are you?

I'm a butterfly.
Who are you?

33

Along came a grasshopper.

Hello, who are you?

I'm a grasshopper. Who are you?

Along came a *snake.*

Hello, who are you?

I'm a snake, and I eat **wide-mouthed** frogs.

Are **you** a **wide-mouthed** frog?

36

37

Tadpole Trouble!

Written by Frances Bacon   Illustrated by Jennifer Cooper

One day, Grandma and Grandpa came
to stay at our house.

38

In the back of their car
was a jar.

In the jar
were twenty tadpoles.

"Tadpoles! How fun!"
I said.
I got a tank.
I put in some water
and some plants.

I put the tadpoles
in the tank.

Uh-oh!
Tadpoles might
mean trouble!

Every day,
I fed my tadpoles.
The tadpoles grew
bigger and bigger.

Then, one day,
I got sick.

I was sad, but
Mum put the tadpoles
in my room.

41

I watched the tadpoles.
They grew and grew.
They grew some legs.
Their tails got smaller.
Their bodies got bigger.

Then, one night... PLOP!
Something wet
was on my head.
I turned on
the light.

There were little frogs everywhere!
"Dad, Dad, come here!"
I cried.

43

Dad opened the door.
"Jeepers creepers!" he shouted.

The frogs jumped past Dad.
Soon we had frogs everywhere.

Mum, Dad, and I
chased the frogs.
We chased them everywhere
until we caught them all.

45

In the morning,
we took the frogs
down to the pond.

We set the frogs free.
"Goodbye, frogs,"
I said, as they hopped away.

46

The next year,
we went to visit
Grandma and Grandpa.

In the back of the car
was a jar.
In the jar
were twenty tadpoles!

Jeepers Creepers

Written by Sarah Irvine   Illustrated by Kelvin Hawley

Wild whacky frogs
all over the place.
Some surf on lily pads
and some play chase.

50

Some play leapfrog.
Some jump on pogo sticks.
Some ride bicycles
and some do tricks.

"Ribbit, ribbit, ribbit,"
comes from a log.
"I'm glad
I'm not a tadpole.
I like being a frog!"

Letters That Go Together

 fr    pr    tr

Sounds I Know

-**ea**   creak, leap

-**ee**   tree, weed

Endings I Know

-**er**   bigger, longer, smaller

Words I Know

along	got	put	was
around	grew	something	were
bigger	hello	their	what
everywhere	live	want	your